Tower Bridge: The History and Legacy of London's Most Iconic Bridge

By Charles River Editors

A 1900 stereocard of Tower Bridge

About Charles River Editors

Charles River Editors is a boutique digital publishing company, specializing in bringing history back to life with educational and engaging books on a wide range of topics. Keep up to date with our new and free offerings with this 5 second sign up on our weekly mailing list, and visit Our Kindle Author Page to see other recently published Kindle titles.

We make these books for you and always want to know our readers' opinions, so we encourage you to leave reviews and look forward to publishing new and exciting titles each week.

Introduction

A modern picture of Tower Bridge

Tower Bridge

"London Bridge is falling down,

Falling down, falling down

London Bridge is falling down,

My fair lady."

For most people, this playful child's rhyme conjures up visions of the tall, majestic, two-towered bridge spanning the River Thames near the Tower of London, with its high footpath providing one of the best views available of the city. The only problem is, this vision is wrong, for the London Bridge of modern times is neither tall nor majestic. Indeed, it is not at all memorable for any reason except for its ability to get the city's commuters back and forth to work each day.

In fact, the tall bridge that symbolizes not just the city but the nation is Tower Bridge, and while it is among the oldest major bridges in London, it is hardly the first to have been built on the Thames, or even on that spot. In actuality, the first men to build a bridge on that spot probably spoke Latin as their first language.

As time passed, technology changed, and with it, the nature of bridge building. Wood gave way to stone, which in turn gave way to iron and steel. At the same, London grew on both land and water, with more people living in and near the city, and more people plying the river in bigger and bigger ships. The people on land needed to get across the river, and the people on the river needed to be able to move along without too much interference. It was obvious that the city needed a new bridge, but years passed before the right design for one came along.

When it finally did, there were still other, non-practical concerns, specifically that the bridge fit in with its surrounding historical environment. In particular, this meant that Londoners wanted to ensure that the bridge's look fit in with the nearby Tower of London. Thus was born a bridge conceived within the marriage of need and desire, strength and beauty. Tower Bridge is unlikely to fall down, or even be torn down, anytime soon, but it is still worthy of singing about.

Tower Bridge: The History and Legacy of London's Most Iconic Bridge examines the long and storied history of one of England's most famous landmarks. Along with pictures depicting important people, places, and events, you will learn about the Tower Bridge like never before.

Tower Bridge: The History and Legacy of London's Most Iconic Bridge
About Charles River Editors
Introduction
   London Bridge and the Need for Other Bridges
   Designing the Tower Bridge
   Building the Bridge
   A Description of the Bridge
   Opening the Bridge
   Online Resources
   Bibliography
Free Books by Charles River Editors
Discounted Books by Charles River Editors

London Bridge and the Need for Other Bridges

When London was debating the construction of the Tower Bridge in its current spot around the end of the 19th century, it was already well-known that bridges had existed there in the past, but it obviously didn't have the history that London Bridge did. In a lecture given in 1893, civil engineer John Wolfe Berry noted, "A bridge appears to have existed on the site, or a few yards lower down the river than the site, of the present London Bridge, from remote antiquity. We read of Canute attacking and being repulsed from London Bridge, and some writers have held that a bridge at this spot dates from the Roman occupation of London, which was then known to the world as the town Augusta, and must have been of considerable importance…Stow says that in the year 994 the Danes were repulsed in an attack which they made on London, because they took no heed of the bridge; but probably there is some misconception here, for it is recorded that only in the previous year Anlaf, the Dane, sailed up the Thames as far as Staines with ninety-three ships and ravaged the country. Discarding the tradition of a Roman bridge, it seems clear that the first London Bridge of which any record exists was erected between the years 993 and 1016, when Canute attacked London a second time, and made a canal on the south side of the river so as to bring his ships past the bridge."

A medieval depiction of Canute the Great

Berry speculated that the first bridge "was probably of wood...the piers being formed of piles driven into the bed of the river, and the openings spanned by timber beams. ... This wooden bridge had great vicissitudes. It was washed away in a flood in 1091, was rebuilt m 1097, and burnt in 1136. It was again rebuilt, but was in so bad a state in 1163 that a new bridge was resolved on, and this time in more durable materials."

It seems that a monk named Peter, then serving as Curate of St. Mary in Colechurch, had at some point in his life trained as a bridge builder. Thus, the Romans hired him to build a new stone bridge near the site, a task that he gave his life to, working on it from 1176-1202. The bridge was finally completed in 1209, but even though stone was obviously sturdier than wood, it was still not permanent, at least not in this case. By 1282, years of freezing and flooding had taken their toll, and large portions of the bridge's support structure had fallen into disrepair.

Instead of replacing the bridge, however, it was repaired and continued to stand for another six centuries. Initially, the bridge's supports were only above 9 feet above the riverbed they were sunk in. As time went only, various builders added more height, including starlings that raised the height of the bridge by another three feet. Perhaps to encourage those who were making pilgrimages, which were treacherous journeys in the Middle Ages, the Chapel of St. Thomas on the Bridge was built at one end of the bridge. This large, rectangular building measured 65 feet long by 20 feet wide but was only about 14 feet tall. Because of its length, it is likely that the chapel extended onto the pier leading to the bridge.

A depiction of the exterior of the chapel

Depictions of the interior

Though it was low, this bridge shared one quality with its descendant in that it had a drawbridge at one end to allow ships to pass through. Of course, this drawbridge was also handy in case of attack, as it could be raised and thus prevent the enemy from using the bridge to cross the river.

Later, in 1426, as England went to war again against France, King Henry VI ordered a tower to be built on the north side of the bridge. This was also a defensive move, as was the decision in 1471 to begin to build small houses on the bridge. This allowed guards to be stationed there permanently for the express purpose of watching for and defending invasion.

Henry VI

Over time, more houses were added, among them Nonsuch House in 1579, one of the most beautiful structures of the time. Writing in *Old and New London, Volume 2*, Walter Thornbury explained, "About the same time was also reared that wonder of London, Nonsuch House—a huge wooden pile, four storeys high, with cupolas and turrets at each corner, brought from

Holland, and erected with wooden pegs instead of nails. It stood over the seventh and eighth arches, on the north side of the drawbridge. There were carved wooden galleries outside the long lines of transom-casements, and the panels between were richly carved and gilt."

Ben Sutherland's picture of a model of Nonsuch House

Three years later, crews of workmen built waterwheels into several of the arches, and they in turn powered a pump to send water into London.

By the early part of the 17th century, there were dozens of homes and other buildings located on what was then known as London Bridge. Then, in 1632, disaster struck when fire broke out and 42 of them were lost. Their owners soon rebuilt, only to be wiped out again during the Great Fire of London in 1666. By this time, the bridge itself had become such an important business district that it could not be abandoned and, by the mid-1670s, new buildings had replaced those lost.

In 1725, some industrious soul took it upon himself to measure the bridge and reported it to be 915 feet long and 73 feet wide, with a road only 20 feet wide running across it. It also sat 43 and a half feet above the water. Because of its height, crossing it proved to be quite a chore, especially for anyone pushing a hand cart or carrying a parcel. However, those living on and near it still considered it state of the art, with one poet writing:

"When Neptune from his billows London spyed,

Brought proudly thither by a high Spring-tide,

As through a floating wood he steered along,

And dancing castles clustered in a throng;

When he beheld a mighty bridge give law

Unto his surges and their fury awe;

When such a shelf of cataracts did roar,

As if the Thames with Nile had changed her shore;

When he such massy walls, such towers, did eye,

Such posts, such irons, upon his back to lye;

When such vast arches he observed, that might

Nineteen Rialtos make for depth and height:

When the Cerulean God these things surveyed,

He shook his trident, and astonished said

Let the whole earth now all the wonders count,

This bridge of wonders is the paramount!"

By the mid-18th Century there was enough traffic on the London Bridge to cause regular problems. Therefore, the government decided to tear down most of the houses on it to widen the road and create two footpaths that would themselves be wide enough to facilitate foot traffic. At the same time, those in charge also began to look for other ways in which the bridge could be improved.

Among the designs submitted was one by the famous architect Sir Christopher Wren. While his was one of the few that actually addressed the problem of navigating under the bridge, it was rejected, along with many others. Instead, the center pier supporting the bridge was removed, widening the passage under it to 70 feet.

Sir Christopher Wren

Unfortunately, this proved to be only a temporary fix, and those in charge of the bridge continued to look for new and better solutions. As a result, in 1824, work began on a new bridge, this one designed by John Rennie and completed by his son, Sir John Rennie the Younger. It took seven years to complete and cost 1.5 million pounds. It was beautiful and elegant, but not terribly serviceable, primarily because it was so steep. Making matters worse, it was never enough, to the extent that by the mid-19th century, Parliament had finally recognized the need for an additional way across the Thames.

An 1832 depiction of the demolition of the Chapel of St. Thomas on the Bridge as part of renovations

John Rennie

Sir John Rennie the Younger

Designing the Tower Bridge

Even as Rennie's bridge was being built, the plan for what would become Tower Bridge was in the works. On December 18, 1824, *The Portfolio* published a proposal for an elevated roadway designed by Sea Captain Samuel Brown, with the help of civil engineer James Walker. 1,000 yards long, it was intended to run from east of the Tower moat to a new dock then being built on the original site of St. Katherine's Hospital. Brown, who had made a fortune by inventing a new and better iron chain, had recently completed work on a chain pier in Brighton.

Historian Denise Silvester-Carr described the proposed design: "The engraving in The Portfolio showed the graceful silhouette of an 80ft high bridge suspended on iron chains between four stone piers. Brown produced figures to indicate that tolls would yield 100 [pounds] a day, but nothing came of this much admired undertaking and 'St Katharine's Bridge of Suspension' -- the future Tower Bridge -- was forgotten for almost fifty years."

In 1876, the Metropolitan Board of Works, in charge of transportation systems in the city, asked Parliament for permission to construct a high level bridge. When completed, their creation would stand on the site of the Tower Bridge. Their proposal called for it to be shaped as a single arch supporting 850 feet of bridge 65 feet above the river. A long, straight road would lead to its north entrance, while its southern entrance would form a spiral. The gradient on each would be a gentle "1 in 40," meaning the road would rise one foot for each 40 feet. The board predicted the new bridge would cost about 1.5 million pounds to build, but that this money could be recovered by the tolls placed on crossing.

In spite of the bridge's height, local ship owners still insisted that it would cause problems for large ships plying the river, while those living near the sites of the north and south entrances complained that the approaches, being around a mile long, would disrupt their lives and neighborhoods. As a result, the plan was ultimately rejected.

Then, in December 1876, *Lloyds Weekly London Newspaper* reported, "At Thursday's meeting of the Court of Common Council a report was brought up from the Special Bridge and Subway committee by Mr. H. A. Isaacs, the chairman, recommending that a bridge over or a subway under the Thames should be constructed eastwaid of London-bridge, and that the most eligible site would be that approached from Little Tower-hill and Irongate Stairs on the north side, and from Horsely-down-lane and stairs on the south-side of the river. The discussion upon the report was postponed until after the vacation."

Some days later, the newspaper *Iron* listed the proposals that had been made thus far for the bridge: "They were attended by all the parties, who were severally heard in relation to and explanation of their respective designs and schemes. They also examined the designs submitted to them by…persons which had not been referred to them by the court…The committee further suggested that they should be authorized to advertise for designs and to offer premiums for those most approved. It was agreed to postpone the discussion until after the meeting, the rival report recommending the widening of the existing bridge being also postponed. Among the private Bills in Parliament for the ensuing session deposited on Saturday was one to enable the Corporation of the City of London, the Metropolitan Board of Works and a company, to be incorporated, to build a bridge on the site recommended by the Bridge and Subway Committee appointed by the Corporation of the City…The cost of the bridge, with approaches, is set down as…370,000 [pounds]. The approach on the City side of the river, it is proposed, shall abut on the new street proposed to be made by the Metropolitan Board of Works. The traffic of the new bridge will be as constant and uninterrupted as that of an ordinary public road, and it is announced that the gradients of its approaches, as well as of the bridge itself, are much easier than those of London Bridge."

Much of the money used to finance the construction of the new bridge came from a unique source: the Bridge House Estates Trust. According to its website, "By the end of the 13th century the shops and houses adorning Peter de Colechurch's new stone London Bridge were beginning to generate not only increased cross-river trade, but also increased taxes, rents and bequests. A significant fund began to accumulate and it was administered from a building on the south side of the bridge called Bridge House, with the fund becoming known as the Bridge House Estates…Over the centuries the fund prospered mightily …. The Bridgemasters maximized income from a great variety of sources including... 'receiving tolls on carts passing over the Bridge, tolls from ships passing under the Bridge and fines for unlawful fishing from the Bridge'. ... In relatively recent years the charity... constructed Tower Bridge."

In addition to monies collected through taxation, the Trust was also gifted through the years with bequests left to "God and the Bridge" by businessmen who had prospered as a result of their location on the bridge. The fund had previously been used to build two other bridges, and now it would finance Tower Bridge.

With that, the committee was given permission to host a public competition to find the best design for the new bridge, but after the search began, it proved to take longer and be more complicated than anyone could have imagined. Writing some years after the bridge was completed, engineer Archibold Williams explained, "Among the many plans submitted since 1867 for a bridge, one is particularly noticeable for its originality — that of Mr. C. Barclay Bruce. He proposed a rolling bridge, to consist of a platform 300 feet long and 100 wide, which should be propelled from shore to shore over rollers placed at the top of a series of piers 100 feet apart. The platform would have a bearing at two points at least, and, according to the designer's calculations, make the journey in three minutes, with a freight of 100 vehicles and 1400 passengers... Another engineer, Mr. F. T. Palmer, proposed a bridge which widened out into a circular form near each shore, enclosing a space into which a vessel might pass by the removal of one side on rollers while traffic continued on the other side. As soon as the vessel had entered the enclosure the sliding platform would be closed again, and that on the other side be opened in turn."

Among those who submitted sketches was Sir Joseph Bazalgette, already known for having designed a number of bridges in and around London, including Maidstone Bridge in 1879. Williams noted that "Bazalgette, engineer to the Metropolitan Board of Works, recommended the construction of a bridge that should give a clear headway of 65 feet above Trinity high-water level, but a Bill brought into Parliament for power to build it was thrown out on the ground that the headway would be insufficient, and on account of the awkward special approaches."

Bazalgette

In spite of his experience, Bazalgette ultimately lost out on his bid to Sir Horace Jones, London's City Architect at the time and, in a blatant example of conflict of interest, one of the judges of the competition. Historian Denise Silvester-Carr observed, "Whether Jones had seen Captain Brown's proposal is not known but in 1878 he suggested that chains should be used to raise the road on a crossing designed to resemble a medieval drawbridge. Twin turrets were deliberately intended to look like the corners of the White Tower at the Tower of London. But the curved steel span would not give sufficient clearance for the bascules...to open fully, and Jones temporarily shelved his 'hasty' plan...Six years later, when a select committee of the House of Commons was discussing the Thames bridges, Jones resurrected the bascule bridge. With the assistance of Sir John Wolfe Barry, the engineer son of the architect of the Houses of Parliament, he submitted a modified scheme. A straight span which would act as a high level walkway was substituted for the arch; hydraulic machinery instead of chains would raise two bascules; lifts would carry passengers up to the walkways and prevent undue delay when ships were passing through."

Jones

Barry

In fact, Jones himself described his bridge as follows: "Apart from the question of appearance and convenience in the passage of vessels, it will render the construction of our road and approaches lighter than in the former bridges, as we should be able to obtain a gradient of 1 in 40 on the south side to the centre of the present level in Tooley Street without any interference with the present level of that street; this would of course give a considerable saving both in compensation and in work. ...the waterway would be obstructed by two piers only of, say, 40 feet each, leaving between them a clear way of 200 feet in the centre; the waterway would therefore be 800 feet at high water mark... foot traffic need not be interrupted even when the bridge is open for the passage of vessels staircases must be constructed for the service of the bridge, and they can, as well as passenger lifts, be so constructed as to serve the public. The convenience to the occupiers or riparian owners, east or west, having nothing before them to interfere with the approach to their wharves, will be an additional advantage, and small craft could pass underneath with greater safety and convenience...."

In October 1884, Barry wrote to Jones, "I have given the subject of the Tower Bridge as much consideration as the time which has been at my disposal since you did me the honour of consulting me would allow. ... With respect to the opening portion of the bridge, I would recommend that the fairway between the tiers of shipping should be kept clear when the bridge is open, and that no centre pier should be permitted...A 'bascule' or lifting bridge would perhaps save some small amount of time in the passage of vessels; it would render the alteration of the level of Tooley Street unnecessary, and would admit of a footway served by hydraulic lifts being practicable from shore to shore, when the bridge was open for river traffic. Further, I see no difficulty, if the latter system be adopted, in spanning the whole of the side openings between the piers on each side of the fairway and the river banks in one span. This would render the construction of side piers unnecessary, and would be a convenience to the side channels…I quite agree with you in the impossibility of making any estimate of the cost at the present moment, but no doubt an approximate estimate might be ready shortly. I may perhaps be permitted to say that any of the three designs shown in the sketches would in my judgment be an ornament to the Port of London."

Barry later explained, "It will be seen that there are two beams balanced on two upright posts, the inner ends of the beams being attached by chains to a hinged platform across the canal, and the outer ends having counter-balance weights on them. As the outer or landward ends of the beams are lowered, the inner ends are raised and pull up the hinged platform and thus open the bridge for the passage of craft…The Bridge House Estates Committee of the Corporation of London…came to the conclusion to recommend the Corporation to…promote a Bill for the erection at the Tower site of a "bascule" bridge as the best means of meeting the case. After the original sketches made by Sir Horace Jones…it was seen that any arched form of construction across the central opening would be very objectionable; as the masts of ships would be in danger of striking the arch unless they were kept exactly in the centre of the span. …we decided that any girders over the central span, when open for the passage of ships, must be horizontal and not arched."

Building the Bridge

The Corporation finally appealed to Parliament in 1885 for permission to authorize the funds to build the bridge. In doing so, it felt that it had finally reconciled the needs of the land traffic with those of the water traffic, the latter primarily as it related to ships going to and from London's famous Upper Pool business district. According to waterways expert Sir Terence Conran, this area, which is located east of the bridge, "is known as the Pool of London, which from Roman times through to the building of enclosed docks in the 19th century accounted for much of the wealth, growth and prominence of London. However, the economic prosperity generated by shipping did not stop the surrounding area from being desperately poor; it was an urban slum that haunted the novels of Charles Dickens from Oliver Twist, his first, to *Our Mutual Friend*, his last…there is Horsleydown Lane, where some say King John was thrown from his horse; the lane lay on the edge of Horsey Downe, a large field used for fairs. Then there is Shad Thames, now the best surviving example of the dramatic canyons formed by warehouses in the area: the name is a corruption of 'St John at Thames', a reference to the period when the area was settled by an Order of the Knights Templar in the 12th century. John Courage's Anchor Brewery was opened in Shad Thames in 1789…"

Given its importance, it is no surprise that the traffic around the Pool of London literally shaped the Tower Bridge, dictating "the general arrangement of the spans of the bridge," specifically with a narrow, approximately 180 feet center opening and two wider side openings, each nearly 300 feet across.

A mid-19th century depiction of the Pool of London

In spite of these plans, the watermen still opposed the bridge, insisting it would hamper their work. The men serving on the Thames Conservancy Board also complained, but their opposition fell on deaf ears as both Houses of Parliament eventually passed the bill authorizing the bridge and specifying the following:

> "(1) A central opening span of 200 feet clear width, with a height of 135 feet above Trinity high water when open, and a height of 29 feet when closed against vessels with high masts. (It may be mentioned in passing that the height of the centre arch of London Bridge is 29 feet above Trinity high water.
>
> (2) The size of the piers to be 185 feet in length and 70 feet in width.
>
> (3) The length of each of the two side spans to be 270 feet in the clear."

At the insistence of the conservators, those working on the bridge had to, at all times, maintain a swath 160 feet wide in the river through which ships and boats could pass. This meant that each of the two piers supporting the bridge had to be built separately.

In spite of these and other delays, on June 21, 1886, work finally began on the bridge. In his opening remarks, the speaker opening the ceremonies reminded his audience of the history of the organization charged with financing the endeavor, saying, "The Corporation of London has possessed for centuries estates charged with the maintenance of London Bridge. These estates were partly bestowed by generous citizens, and partly derived from gifts made at the Chapel of St. Thomas a Becket on London Bridge, for the maintenance of the bridge…the Committee charged with the management of the Bridge House Estates brought up to the Court, by the hand of their chairman, Mr. Frank Green, in 1884, a full and exhaustive report, with plans, recommending that application be made to Parliament for powers to construct a new bridge across the River Thames from the Tower; which was agreed to. In the Session of 1885, the same Committee, under the chairmanship of Mr. Thomas Beard, successfully promoted a Bill in Parliament authorizing the construction of a bridge…Its completion within the space of four years…will supply a paramount need that has been sorely felt by dwellers and workers on the north and south sides of the Thames below London Bridge, and at the same time will greatly relieve the congested traffic across that ancient and famous thoroughfare."

For its part, the *Echo* reported, "The much-discussed, long-delayed Tower Bridge is to take definite shape at last. The work will be commenced this evening by the Prince of Wales, and in due time it will be possible for the road traffic between Limehouse and Deptford, or Shadwell and Rotherhithe, to escape the long, weary round by London Bridge. The wonder is that East London has put up with the inconvenience so long…To the North of that long stretch of bridgeless river there is a population equal to that of Liverpool, Manchester, and Glasgow rolled into one. To the South there is another great and growing population that has suffered seriously for want of communication with the North side. It has never been denied that it was possible to bridge the Thames below London-bridge. In a well-governed city the step would have been taken long ago; but experience of the City Corporation and the Metropolitan Board of Works has taught the East-end to subdue its natural aspirations, and to expect nothing, so that it should not be disappointed…At last, after a more than usually prolonged talking stage, East London is to have a substitute for the Thames Subway. We congratulate the fifteen hundred thousand people on the promised possession of a bridge. We congratulate the City Corporation on being able to make up its mind. We congratulate the frequenters of London-bridge on the prospect of a relief from the congestion of traffic that great commercial highways resents; and if certain civic officials are to make a fortune out of it, that no more than others have done before them."

Oblivious to the controversy surrounding the new construction, or more likely just choosing to ignore it, Albert Edward, the Prince of Wales and future King Edward VII, marked the occasion by proclaiming, "It gives the Princess of Wales and myself sincere pleasure to be permitted on behalf of the Queen, my dear mother, to lay the first stone of the New Tower Bridge. In her name, we thank you for your loyal address, and assure you of her interest in this great undertaking. All must allow that this work, when completed, will be one of great public utility and general convenience, as tending materially to relieve the congested traffic across this noble river. We shall always retain in our remembrance this important ceremony."

Edward VII

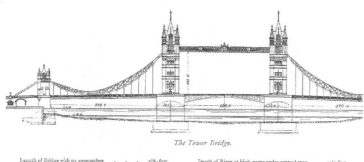

The Tower Bridge.

A model of the bridge

According to the *London Herald*, "As the cheers with which the conclusion of the speech of the Prince subsided, his Royal Highness advanced to the stone and placed in a cavity a bottle containing plans, coins, and newspapers of the date. The memorial stone was then lowered to its bed, and the Prince, after trying it with line and plummet, pronounced it well and truly laid... The sword and mace were then placed in saltire on the stone, and the Bishop of London read a dedicatory prayer, part of which was lost to the majority of the spectators in the booming of the guns from the adjoining battery giving forth a Royal salute. At the close of the prayer, the Chairman of the Bridge House Estates Committee, Architect, Engineer, and other gentlemen were presented to their Royal Highnesses, the first-named, Mr. Atkinson, on behalf of the Corporation, presenting the Princess with a diamond pendant in commemoration of the event... This little ceremony concluded, the National Anthem was sung by the choir of the Guildhall School of Music, and the Royal party were conducted to the entrance to the Tower by the Constable and other officers, and took their departure a midst enthusiastic cheers. Inside the Tower Gates the Coldstream Guards lined the route to the pavilion, where a guard of honour of the same regiment was stationed. The warders of the Tower were stationed inside the entrance to the pavilion."

The stone itself was inscribed,

THIS MEMORIAL STONE

WAS LAID BY

H.R.H. ALBERT EDWARD PRINCE OF WALES, K.G.,

ON BEHALF OF HER MAJESTY QUEEN VICTORIA,

ON MONDAY, THE 21ST JUNE, 1886,

IN THE 50TH YEAR OF HER MAJESTY'S LONG, HAPPY, AND PROSPEROUS REIGN.

THE RIGHT HON. JOHN STAPLES, Lord Mayor.

DAVID EVANS, ESQ RE, Alderman [and] Thos. Clarke, Esq. RE, Sheriffs

EDWARD ATKINSON, ESQ RE, Chairman of the Bridge House Estates Committee.

HORACE JONES, ESQ RE, City Architect.

JOHN WOLFE BARRY, ESQ RE, Engineer.

In order to facilitate the bridge's construction, and to mollify the watermen, the government allowed the builders to use a small portion of the famous Tower Ditch to construct the northern approach to the bridge. In return, the architect agreed to build the bridge in such a way as to coordinate with the ancient style and grace of the Tower of London.

Bob Collowan's picture of the Tower of London

The piers themselves are unique in that they contain the mechanisms necessary to open and close the bridge. On November 8, 1893, a reporter writing for the *Echo* had the opportunity to go deep into the bowels of the bridge. The reporter wrote, "The light of a match showed a faint gleam of water in the gulf below. There were nine feet of it, in fact—not from the river; that flowed in its bed far above us, for the foundations of the Tower Bridge go seventy feet below the bed of the Thames, and we were in one of the buttresses." He continued, "The water— fresh, clear, and potable—bubbled from a spring that had been struck in digging out a foothold for the huge structure whose mass of stone and iron towered hundreds of feet overhead, for the summits of the towers are 275 feet above Trinity water-mark, and we were a long way beneath the keels of the ships, and the flowing channel in which they rode...We retraced our steps along the bricked tunnel into the counterpoise pit. You do not see any bricks about the Tower Bridge from the outside; there are 31,000,000 of them nevertheless. Another thing you do not see is the mighty framework—the bones of steel and iron--for the stone casing of the towers is little more than an ornamental skin. You do see the ponderous chains interlocked in double festoons; but you do not see the anchors with which they grip the earth 45 feet underground."

After descending those 45 feet, he described the sight: "There are 350 tons of...lead for the counterpoise, and, of course, the same quantity in the pit on the other side. Looking upwards, there was a sweep of mighty cogs, and the ponderous ends of the bascule, which, with its fellow, will bridge the space of 200 feet between the towers, and when a steamer wants to pass through, will fly back against the face of the tower with as little trouble as if it were the lid of a watch, though not so rapidly."

The first step in building the piers was to construct heavy duty iron and wood caissons that could be sunk into the riverbed. One article described these in detail for readers: "The caissons used for securing the foundation of the piers consisted of strong boxes of wrought iron, without either top or bottom. To secure a good foundation it was found necessary to sink them to a depth of about 21 feet into the bed of the river. There were twelve caissons for each pier. On the north and south sides of each pier was a row of four caissons, each 28 feet square, joined at either end by a pair of triangular caissons, formed approximately to the shape of the finished pier...The caissons enclosed a rectangular space 34 feet by 124½ feet. The space was not excavated until the permanent work forming the outside portion of the pier had been built, in the caissons and between them, up to a height of 4 feet above high-water mark...First came the building of the caisson upon wooden supports over the site where it was to be sunk. The caisson was 19 feet in height and it was divided horizontally into two lengths. The lower portion was known as the permanent caisson and the upper portion, which was removable when the pier was completed, was called the temporary caisson. The object of this upper portion was simply to keep out water while the pier was being built...When ready the supports were removed and the permanent caisson lowered to the riverbed (this had previously been levelled by divers) by means of four powerful screws attached to four lowering rods. After the caisson had reached the ground various lengths of temporary caisson were added to the permanent section, till the top of the temporary portion came above the level of high water."

Unfortunately, each time time a caisson was lowered, there was a danger that something might go wrong, and eventually something did. According to J.E. Tuit, an engineer for Sir William

Arrol and Co., "The first was due to the removal of some moorings from near the site of one of the square caissons at the north pier, which had left a hole…and, after two days of tide-work, the water was excluded. Two more days had passed…when…the water rushed in through a rent in the clay, which extended to a depth of about 9in. below the cutting edge. … The temporary caisson was therefore made 2ft. higher by a couple of timbers bolted all round the top, and the sinking was continued by divers to a depth of 11 ft. below the ordinary level. … The sluices were then opened, and three days were allowed for the concrete to set before the water in the caisson was again pumped out…The second blow took place in one of the angle caissons at the south pier, and was due to a stage pile in the narrow space between the two angle caissons being driven in a slanting direction so that, as the caisson went down, its cutting edge came in contact with the pile, and thus loosened the clay in the immediate neighborhood. … The adjoining angle caisson had been previously sunk, and the blow being in the space between the two, all danger of another mishap was averted by driving the piles and removing the water from the narrow space between them, before again pumping."

Once these rooms were in place, pumps extracted the water from them and created an environment in which men could dig into the riverbed to pour the foundations for the piers. As they dug, the men continued to shore up the caissons, working to a depth of more than 50 feet below the surface of the river. In 1888, *Iron* reported, "There caissons are filled with Portland cement concrete up to the top to a certain level and from that point upwards the piers are constructed of Cornish and brickwork in Portland cement. On each each of the piers a lofty tower will be erected, the top which will receive the Upper ends of the suspension chains of the side spans, and will also support the high level foot bridge across the central opening."

In spite of these and other setbacks, progress continued until the piers actually reached the fetid air that hovered above the Thames during the Victorian Era. In order to make this moment possible, the men digging in the caissons had moved more than 30,000 cubic yards of mud and clay from the bottom of the mighty river and replaced it with even more cement, bricks and Cornish granite. A few days later, those watching the progress could clearly see the two mammoth piers that would soon support the mighty towers that would make the bridge an icon. Each one was guaranteed to hold more than 70,000 tons of steel and stone, not to mention the heavy iron works of the bridge itself. Finally, each pier, as it emerged from the riverbed itself, was faced with Cornish granite slabs, each more than two feet thick.

With the piers in place, it was time to begin construction on the towers themselves, and soon an advertisement appeared proclaiming, "Notice is hereby given that the Bridge House Estate Committee of the Corporation of London will MEET at Guildhall, on FRIDAY, the 10th day of May next, to receive TENDERS for the SUPPLY, DELIVERY, AND ERECTION OF THE IRON AND STEEL WORK OF THE SUPERSTRUCTURE OF THE TOWER BRIDGE. Drawings and specification may be seen at the office of Mr. J. Wolfe Barry, the engineer of the bridge…and copies of the drawings, specification, quantities, and form of Tender may be obtained there on loan, on deposit of one hundred pounds, which, except in the case of the contractor whose Tender is accepted, will be returned to all who tend in a bonifide Tender and return all the documents." It was signed, "JOHN A. BRAND, Comptroller of the Bridge House Estates. Guildhall, 2nd April 1889.

A few months later, in July 1889, *Lloyd's Weekly Newspaper* reported, "At a meeting of the Court of Common council, held at the Guildhall on Thursday, the Lord Mayor presiding, contracts were sealed between the corporation and Messrs. Arrol and Biggart for the construction of the iron and steel work of the superstructure of the Tower Bridge for the sum of 337,113 [pounds] and between Mr. H. H. Bartlett and the corporation for the construction of the masonry, brickwork, and carpentry of the superstructure of the same bridge for 149,122 [pounds]. In reply to questions, Mr. John Cox said the original estimate for the first-mentioned works was 250,000 [pounds... In the towers there will be hydraulic lifts for giving foot passengers access to the high-level footway, and stairs will also be provided. The mode of actucating the two leaves of the bridge will be by rotary hydraulic engines, acting through gearing on four quadrant racks applied to the rear ends of the bridge. The contract for the hydraulic machinery actuating the lifting portions of the bridge will be carried out by Sir William Armstrong, II & Co. of Elswick, who have, in conjunction Mr. Barry, worked out all the details of the machinery... The steam engines for actuating, the hydraulic machinery will be placed on the southern side of the river beneath and adjoining southern approach to the bridge. They will consist of engines of 360 horsepower each, taking steam from four boilers. Four of the accumulators will be placed upon the piers and two upon the south side of the river. The weight of steel and iron in the chain girders will be about 7,000 tons. Each of the bridge will weigh about 350 tons. The superarea of each leaf will be about 5,000 square feet."

A picture of the bridge being constructed

A Description of the Bridge

Tower Bridge in 1900

The Tower of London and Tower Bridge in the early 20th century

When completed, the bridge was covered in 235,000 cubic feet of stonework, part of it Cornish granite and the rest Portland stone. Underneath were 31 million bricks, 70,000 cubic yards of concrete, 20,000 tons of cement, and 14,000 tons of iron and steel. It was built in three parts, with suspension bridges on either side held up by heavy chains anchored to land and then draped over abutment towers. At their tallest, the chains reach more than 140 feet above the water line. In the center is a pair of high level walkways that give those with the courage to walk them an amazing view of the river and the city. The lower level of the center features a drawbridge that can open to allow tall ships to pass through.

Of course, the most spectacular part of the bridge is its pair of tall towers, each with an octagonal column at each of its four corners. Each column is more than five feet across and more than 100 feet tall and rose from atop a huge, watertight piece of granite, to which it was affixed with giant bolts holding it to the pier itself. The first landing stands 60 feet above the foundational piers and supports that bascule bridge. The second landing is 28 feet above it, and the third landing is another 28 feet up and opens onto the two upper walkways.

A modern picture of the towers

In the late 1930s, *Wonders of World Engineering* explained the special concerns caused by covering steel with stone: "It was important that precautions should be taken to prevent any adhesion between the masonry and the steelwork of the towers. With this object the columns were covered with canvas as the masonry was built round them, and spaces were left in places where any later deformation of the steelwork might bring undue weight upon the adjacent stonework. The masonry covering forms an excellent protection against extremes of temperature. All parts of the metal not accessible for painting purposes after the bridge was completed were coated thoroughly with Portland cement...Manholes were provided in the steel columns to make it possible to paint the interior whenever it became necessary. The abutments of the bridge, which were built by means of cofferdams in the usual manner and without difficulty, have similar but shorter towers."

Then there was the matter of the walkways. The article continued, "These are cantilever structures, each with a suspended span. They were built out from either tower simultaneously. The footways are cantilevers for a distance of 55 feet from either tower and suspended girders for the remaining distance of 120 feet between the cantilever ends." Furthermore, "Along the upper boom of the footway run the great ties connecting the suspension chains at their river ends. Each of the two ties is 301 feet long and is composed of eight plates 2 feet deep and 1 inch thick, ending in large eye-plates to take the pins uniting them to the suspension chains...Each chain is composed of two parts, or links, the shorter dipping from the top of the abutment tower to the roadway, the longer rising from the roadway to the summit of the main tower. The links have each a lower and upper boom, connected by diagonal bracing so as to form a rigid girder. They were built in the positions they had to occupy, supported on trestles, and were not freed until they had been joined by huge steel pins to the ties crossing the central span and to those on the abutment towers."

For all its beauty, the bridge could never have been built had it not been able to open and close to allow river traffic to pass through. Each of the two leaves that could open to an 86 degree angle is about 160 feet long and weigh more than 1,000 tons. In 1907, one reporter noted, "Few enterprises have more completely justified their existence than the Tower Bridge. The bascules open and shut so easily, that the hydraulic lifts for passengers, says the 'Daily News,' are hardly used at all, for every one prefers to watch the ships go by and wait until the roadway swings into its place again. So absorbing has this amusement apparently become, that the Monument has gone quite melancholy over the falling-off in its receipts...The country cousins who were generally good for at lease some £120 a month, now despise clambering up its stone steps to pay three pence for a grimy view, when they can go up to the Tower Bridge for nothing, and have a far finer sight from the high level footway. So true is it, that when your British public can get a thing for nothing in one place, it will not pay a cent in another for a similar enjoyment."

C.M. Lee's picture of a tall ship going through the bridge

The process was, and is, something to see. For one thing, there was the matter of where the power to move the giant leaves would come from. On the south side of the river near the bridge was a simple looking building that served a mighty purpose, for inside it were housed two large pools holding the water that would be called into use to open and close the bridge. When pressed into service, the water shot out of its tank under 700 to 800 pounds of pressure per square inch.

Since the ability to move ships past the bridge was critical, as was the ability to lower the bridge and restore street traffic, Tower Bridge had not one but two engines, one on each side of the river. Both could do the jobs necessary to keep the bridge operational, so there was always a backup. Likewise, the bridgehouse was always guarded against unwelcome intruders who might tamper with its mechanisms, which is understandably of great comfort to anyone who has ever crossed a drawbridge and had a fleeting fear it might open under their feet. Fortunately, there was more than one method of prevention for this; for example, when the bridge was down, the leaves locked together with bolts powered by hydraulic energy, ensuring that even if something went wrong with the mechanics controlling the bridge, they would still lock gently together.

One of the original steam engines

Of course, what was perhaps most amazing was the speed with which the bridge could be raised and lowered. From the moment the first gear began to turn to raise the bridge, through the time it took for a ship to pass, to the time that the bridge was lowered and normal traffic patterns were restored, less than five minutes would pass. Likewise, the lifts, each of which could carry up to 18 passengers to the walkway more than 10 stories above, took less than one minute. One can almost imagine Victorian gentlemen in top hats pulling out their pocket watches to time how long it took the bridge to open and close on any given occasion and nodding in approval each time the bridge master shaved a few seconds off his previous time.

Opening the Bridge

The big day finally came on July 2, 1894. That afternoon, all sorts of pageantry commemorated the official opening of the Tower Bridge. One paper described the affair: "Many and splendid as have been the pageants witnessed in the City of London during its long Municipal life, few have been more brilliant, or will have a more abiding and historic interest, than that of Saturday last, when the Prince of Wales, on behalf of the Queen, opened the great Tower Bridge, which is one of the latest undertakings that the people of the Metropolis owe to the public spirit of the Cooperation. The occasion was one which drew together all classes in a common fellowship... It gratified the popular desire for spectacular display; it emphasized once more the value of the services rendered by the ancient Corporation to the commerce and industry of London; and it furnished the opportunity for such an expression of loyalty towards the Royal family as has not often been surpassed in the City annals. The day was ideally perfect in the all-important matter of the weather, the arrangements were admirably conceived and carried out, and the Royal procession from Marlborough House to the Bridge, and the return by water, was one long ovation of the most gratifying and enthusiastic kind."

In his speech, the Prince of Wales declared, "It is a great satisfaction to the Princess of Wales and myself to be permitted on behalf of the Queen, my dear mother, to open the Tower Bridge across the River Thames, and we thank you for your loyal and dutiful address on the occasion. This Bridge will be an enduring monument of the well-directed energy and public spirit of the Corporation of London; it will also serve as an example of the splendid engineering skill bestowed on its construction...Linking two busy and populous districts of the Metropolis, the Bridge will afford immediately increased facilities of communication, and be of the greatest service to the industrious inhabitants of these districts; while from its ingenious and admirable arrangement it will not interfere with the navigation of the river."

The plague commemorating the auspicious day read simply, "This Bridge was opened by HRH the Prince of Wales, KG on behalf of Her Majesty Queen Victoria, on Saturday the 30th June 1894 in the presence of HRH The Princess of Wales, HRH The Duke of York KG and other members of the Royal Family, the Right Honorable Sir George Robert Tyler, Bart., Lord Mayor." Below this inscription were 43 names, including "2 Sheriffs, 1 Engineer, 8 Members of the Bridge House Estates Committee, 31 Commoners and 1 Comptroller of the Bridge House Estates."

Despite the great fanfare, not everyone was thrilled with the bridge. On July 31, the wire services reported, "Thomas Cantwell and Charles Quinn, two anarchists charged with inciting persons, to murder members of the royal family on the day preceding the opening of the Tower bridge, are on trial at the Old Bailey. The prisoners, it appears, the day before the opening of the Tower bridge, succeeded in getting together a crowd about them on Tower Hill."

The article went on to relate how Cantwell mounted the parapet of a wall and displayed a placard that read, "Tower Bridge Fellow Workers:—You have expended life, energy and skill in building this bridge. Now come the royal vermin and, the rascally politicians, with pomp and splendor, to claim all the credit. You are condemned to the workhouse and paupers' graves to glorify these lazy swine who live upon our labor. I heard men saying 'leave tears and praying. The sharp knife heedeth not the sheep.' Are we not stronger than the rich?'"

Unfortunately, anarchists were not the only ones who marred the joyous atmosphere brought about by the new bridge. Less than two months after it opened, the *Westminster Budget* ran an article aptly titled, "A STUDY IN SUICIDE". It began, "It is difficult to understand why the

Tower Bridge should have so rapidly come into favour that it already rivals Waterloo Bridge as a popular suicide resort. But it certainly has done so, for already, during the brief time which has elapsed since its opening, five men have dropped from its heights into the river below."

The author then quoted a policeman stationed on the bridge, who opined, "I cannot see why men who want to commit suicide should select this bridge to do it from. The only thing that suggests itself to me is the novelty of the idea—and that will not last long at this rate. There may be one other point. People read that another man has 'jumped off the Tower Bridge' and they at once run away with the idea that the attempted suicide took place from off the high footway…That is nonsense—nobody can get off that footway. It is from the lower level bridge that the men have jumped— though even that is high enough—and they have been lucky in not hurting themselves in the fall, although they were prevented from drowning. But if it were possible for a man to go off the high bridge, he would be almost sure to break half the bones in his body in the fall."

In answer to the question, "Is there anything about this bridge, then, to tempt a man to suicide?" the bobby responded, "No, of course not. But if a man were looking for a chance to commit suicide, I could quite understand his preferring this bridge to any other. In my opinion a great many of the attempts at suicide are made on the impulse of the moment. You know that a man standing on a great height often has a giddy feeling, and has to hold himself back almost to prevent himself from jumping over. Well, I think it is something like that here…A man leans over the parapet, as he is crossing the bridge, to watch the water rushing through underneath. The parapet is low, and instead of being an enormous wall of stone, it is just a nicely-polished wooden rail. He feels some sudden impulse and over he goes. Of course there are 'drunks' and men who are sick of starving—I can understand why they go over. But I think my idea is right in many cases."

The article finally concluded, "Whatever may be the incentive to jump over, the act is being guarded against with great care. There were quite half-a-dozen policemen posted on the bridge while our informant was explaining his view of the situation, and they appeared to have nothing at all to do, so they may have been told off simply to interfere with intending suicides."

Once the bridge was completed, it had to be maintained. In 1910, less than 15 years after it opened for business, some repairs had to be made. According to one reporter at the time, "Naturally a great deal of money has to be paid out each year for repairs, and some idea of this may be given by referring to the cost of repainting Tower bridge about a couple of years ago. One hundred men were engaged on the work night and day and to give three coats of paint to every inch of the ironwork required about sixty tons of paint. Miles of scaffolding were erected to make the work safe: but, at the same time, the men employed were covered by special insurance…Besides the illumination given by carbide lamps of 2500 candlepower, hundreds of pounds of candles were used nightly by the workmen. Gilding the large crestings of the bridge, and the city arms and shields on the footways cost $2000, while the total cost was about $30,000. The interval allowed between each painting of the bridge is six years, so that for this work alone the expenditure on Tower bridge is $5,000 a year."

The turn of the 20th century brought with it all kinds of new technology, especially in the world of travel. Airplanes were seen more and more often in the skies above London and other large cities as pilots tried one new trick after another, and inevitably, the Tower Bridge became a prop for one man's exploits. On August 12, 1912, the *London Standard* told readers about one such stunt: "A British airman, Mr. F. K. McClean, on a British hydro-aeroplane (a Short) has gained the honour of being the first aviator to fly up the Thames to Westminster and to alight on the river after skimming the water and passing under the arches of several of the bridges. ... Mr. McClean arrived shortly before 8 o'clock, and was first seen like a speck between but away beyond the towers of Tower Bridge. At first many of the spectators refused to believe that the object was an aeroplane."

For his part, McClean recalled, "I just thought I'd come. I had an engagement in London at midday, and I've done the journey from Eastchurch, 68 miles, in 80 minutes. ... At first I was not sure what to do in the case of the Tower Bridge, but when I get to it I went between the roadway and the upper footway. You see, the arches of the bridges are big things when you get near to them."

For all that the Tower Bridge today represents London to people around the world, it has not always been popular. At the time of its completion in 1894, *The Builder* complained that the towers gave "the appearance of carrying immense suspension chains which they could not possibly carry. The writer added, "Although the masonry towers are only envelopes and could not possibly carry the chains which appear to be suspended across them, they have as least the aspect of being solidly built towers founded on the piers which carry the bridge. But even this is a delusion. Will it be credited that these masonry towers are actually built on and carried by the ironwork; their side walls have no foundations at all—they are slung, as it were in gigantic stirrups of steel, and at the period of our visit to the works you could actually look under the base of the walls into a vacant space above which they were banging... What will be the ultimate result of the masonry of this depending on a large steel structure which must be subject to constant movement future years will have to show. What strikes one at present is that the whole structure is the most monstrous and preposterous architectural sham that we have ever known of, and is in that sense a discredit to the generation which has erected it... Far better would it have been to have built simply the naked steal work, and let the construction show us what it really is: the effect, if somewhat bare looking, would have been at least honest and we should have been relieved from the spectacle of many thousands spent on what is not the bridge at all—what is no part of its structure—but an elaborate and costly make-believe."

Likewise, in 1916, architect H. H. Stratham complained, "The Tower Bridge... represents the vice of tawdriness and pretentiousness, and of falsification of the actual facts of the structure. It is stated that the exterior clothing was designed by an architect; he cannot have been a very eminent one, as we never hear his name; it looks to me more like what results from the advertisement we sometimes see –'Wanted immediately a draughtsman; must be an expert Gothic hand'- - it is draughtsman's architecture…The exceedingly heavy suspension chains are made to appear to hang on an ornamental stone structure which they would in reality drag down, and the side walls of the apparently solid tower rest on part of the iron structure, and you could see under them before the roadway was made up. All architects would have much preferred the plain steel structure to this kind of elaborate sham. The same kind of spirit is showing itself in the treatment of ironwork; capitals inserted where they have nothing to do with the structure, spandrils filled in with bad Gothic tracery, and so on. If iron is designed on good lines, it will look better in itself without these gewgaws."

Stratham later softened his remarks, saying, "Sir Horace Jones's design would have been better for greater simplicity, and especially for the omission of the unnecessary and trivial projecting bay windows or oriels at the sides in the lower portion. But in the main it is a fine and massive design, with a good deal of character about it, and it had the merit of being really what it pretended to be—a solid masonry tower." Nonetheless, he couldn't help but take more shots at the bridge: "When the engineer came to the unfortunate decision to make the towers a sham skin of masonry hiding a real construction of steel, after Sir Horace Jones's death, the design was put into the hands of another architect… He may have received orders merely to modify Sir Horace Jones's design; and people who know nothing of architectural detail may think it only amounts to that…But every architect can see that the result is that, while one or two weak points in Sir Horace Jones's design have been retained, every good quality it had has been re moved and the whole thing hopelessly vulgarised. It is therefore absurd, and a gross injustice to Sir Horace Jones, to speak of the towers as they now stand as his design. As I said before, they are specimens of draughtsman's architecture."

Stratham also quoted J. E. Tuit, who had served as an engineer for the contractors, as saying, "On comparing it with the structure which has now been completed, it will be seen that so many modifications have been made that practically only the principle of Mr. Jones's early design has been retained." Stratham insisted, however, that, "In a structural sense, even the principle has not been retained; but the remark forms a strong independent testimony to the truth of my statement that the towers as now erected cannot be regarded as Sir Horace Jones's design, and that it is absurd to call them so."

Due to its fame and prominence, Tower Bridge often finds itself at the center of some sort of protest, the most dangerous and dramatic of which occurred in 1968. On April 5 of that year, the *Associated Press* reported, "A jet fighter plane buzzed the House of Commons twice at noon Friday and then flew under the upper part of Tower Bridge, skimming only feet above the busy traffic. … The pilot flew between the two towers and between the roadway and footway." It was later determined that the pilot, Alan Pollock, pulled the stunt to protest the lack of aerial displays at the RAF's 50 year anniversary celebration. He later admitted that he never set out to fly through the bridge: "Until this very instant I'd had absolutely no idea that, of course, Tower Bridge would be there. It was easy enough to fly over it, but the idea of flying through the spans suddenly struck me. I had just ten seconds to grapple with the seductive proposition which few ground attack pilots of any nationality could have resisted. My brain started racing to reach a decision. Years of fast low-level strike flying made the decision simple…"

A 1950s picture of a Royal Air Force plane in the river with the Tower Bridge behind it

In the years following World War II, many of the warehouses near the river closed, making Tower Bridge less necessary, so in an effort to shore up its commercial appeal, the Corporation began a long, arduous process to rebrand the bridge as a tourist destination. In 1975, the Board replaced the steam engines with electric motors, modernizing the way in which both the drawbridge and the lifts operated. It also began to explore the possibility of reopening the walkways.

Initially, many opposed their efforts, claiming that the walkways were a nuisance that attracted those contemplating suicide, but when one considers the number of people who use the bridge each year, there have been a surprisingly small number of suicides. Ultimately, this problem was solved by enclosing the formerly open walkways in glass in 1982. The *Associated Press* reported, "Tower Bridge, the sturdy landmark over the Thames, has reopened for the first time in 7 years in a celebration of Victorian durability and eccentricity. ... Now the walkways and the floor below in both towers are thronged by tourists who come for the view, and to see exhibits about the bridge's history, including its still operational original lifting mechanism. ...2,000 to 3,000 people a day are visiting the reopened towers."

John Fielding, then the tourist manager for the bridge, added, "It's London's Eiffel Tower. There's nothing quite like it in the world. Certainly there are bigger and more splendid bridges, but this is unique, the most instantly recognizable." Concerning why it had ever been closed, explained, "Pedestrians soon found it was too much effort to climb up those stairs when the drawbridge was open, especially since the bridge mechanism can open and close in under six minutes. The walkways became a haven for derelicts, so they were closed to the public and only reopened with the renovation completed last June 30."

The interior of the walkway

One of the most amazing events in the bridge's history took place in the post-war years. According to writer David Ellis, "AS EVENING began falling across London on December 30, 1952, bus driver Albert Gunter must have wondered if he'd lapsed into a nightmare as he started driving his Number 78 bus across Tower Bridge straddling the River Thames. For the centre of the bridge comprises two 30m-long hinged bascules (or leaves) that open upwards at over 80 degrees to allow ships to pass through. To his horror, the one he was on was rising at an increasingly sickening angle right under his bus and its 20 passengers... Making a split-second decision, Albert dropped two gears and gunned the engine of the cumbersome double-decker as fast as it would go - miraculously leaping the vehicle forward from the bascule, and somehow 'flying' it through mid-air to drop, deafeningly but still upright, almost two metres down on to the opposite leaf that had not yet begun to rise. His conductor suffered a broken leg, 12 passengers received minor injuries, and Albert himself was given a 10-pound reward for his heroics... with a subsequent inquiry finding the bascule had been raised due to a mix-up between staff."

In April 2011, *The Evening Standard* of London reported on the status of the bridge ahead of the approaching 2012 Summer Olympics:

> "TOWER Bridge, one of London's most prominent landmarks, is to undergo a lighting makeover. An energy-efficient system will be installed before the Olympics to help reduce energy bills and cut carbon emissions. It will also enhance the world-famous structure's architectural features at night. Tower Bridge's gothic turrets, central aerial walkway and suspension chains will be bathed in colours sensitive to its listed building status.
>
> "The lighting system... will be flexible so the intensity of light, as well as the colours, can be varied. This means, for example, that it could be spectacularly lit up in the colours of the Union Jack during the 2012 Games. The bridge currently has traditional, static floodlighting which can flatten the architecture and has not been upgraded for 25 years. The makeover, which follows major repainting work, will be funded at no cost to the taxpayer by energy firms EDF and GE and the bridge's owner, the City of London Corporation."

Along with the rest of the nation, Boris Johnson, who arranged the transformation, insisted, "I want London to look its very best in 2012 as the eyes of the world are upon us. Tower Bridge is one of this city's most stunning landmarks, recognized the world over and therefore deserving of a star role in these year-long celebrations. I am thrilled to have brokered this deal to bathe Tower Bridge in ecofriendly light to create a fresh perspective of this wonderful icon. This is another great legacy for London stretching for decades beyond the Olympic year."

A picture of Tower Bridge during the 2012 Olympics

By this time, many Londoners had become completely dependent on the bridge to complete their morning commutes. That is why there was such an outcry when word came it would have to be closed for repairs. *The Evening Standard* told readers, "TOWER BRIDGE will be shut to traffic for three months from October 1 amid warnings of gridlock on both sides of the Thames. The Victorian landmark will be closed to vehicles and bicycles while it undergoes maintenance. Black cab drivers calculate that even the shortest river crossing could take up to 30 minutes longer at peak times. Works being undertaken include replacing the decking on the bridge's bascules plus removing rust, mechanical repairs and road resurfacing…More than 40,000 motorists and pedestrians cross Tower Bridge every day. Pedestrians will also be banned from the bridge for three weekends during the works, with the possibility of a free ferry to move them across the river. Cabbies today questioned the timing of the works. But the City of London Corporation said this was because it is when the Thames is quietest for riverboat traffic." In spite of the outcry, Chris Hayward, the head of London's planning and transport committee, insisted: "This decision to close Tower Bridge has not been taken lightly. We will use this time to repair, refurbish, and upgrade London's most iconic bridge, which has gone without significant engineering works for more than 35 years."

In 1993, as the bridge approached its 100 year anniversary, those in charge created a special exhibition chronicling the first century of the bridge's history. There were videos showing grainy black and white photographs of the bridge as it rose up above the Thames, as well as animatronic workmen explaining their hardships in building the marvel. There were also exhibit cases full of machinery, as well as large panels giving details about the logistics behind constructing the bridge.

Today, according to the Tower's website, the exhibition continues: "Tower Bridge Exhibition is the most exciting way to explore the most famous bridge in the world. From the modern high-level Walkways and its spectacular new glass floor to the historic Engine Rooms and towers; Tower Bridge Exhibition tells the history of the bridge explaining how and why it came into existence. By way of our grand Victorian staircase or fully accessible lift, visitors are invited to travel back in time to the nineteenth century. From the North tower, explore the fascinating history of Tower Bridge: its significance and its function; its place in history and in the heart of the nation... A short bespoke video shown by artist, Stephen Biesty, depicting the construction of the Bridge can be enjoyed in the South Tower before wandering down the beautiful staircase, complemented by 'Battersea to Bermondsey', LED-lit motion sensitive artworks showing iconic buildings along the Thames. The experience culminates in a visit to the Victorian Engine Rooms, which houses one of London's true hidden gems: huge and beautifully maintained steam engines, furnaces and accumulators that were once used to power the raising of Tower Bridge's 'bascules' – the moveable roadways at the bridge's centre. Exciting hands-on mechanisms and information panels will explain the ingenious hydraulic technology used over the years to keep the bridge in motion."

For those with a more adventurous spirit, the website informs readers, "Moving through to the high-level Walkways, visitors will be able to experience our biggest and most exciting development to the Exhibition since it originally opened: the Glass Floor – a unique viewpoint of London life. Make sure to plan your visit for the chance to see the magic of the bridge lifting beneath your feet!" At the same time, visitors who prefer not to look down can still "admire stunning panoramic views from the Walkways, spying popular London landmarks such as St Paul's Cathedral and the Monument to the west and St Katharine Docks leading to Canary Wharf to the east."

Online Resources

Other books about English history by Charles River Editors

Other books about Tower Bridge on Amazon

Bibliography

Barry, John Wolfe. (1894) *The Tower Bridge: A Lecture.*

Billington, David P. (1985) *The Tower and the Bridge: The New Art of Structural Engineering.*

Speaker-Yuan, Margaret. (2004) *The London Tower Bridge.*

Tuit, James Edward. (1894) *The Tower Bridge: Its History and Construction from the Date of the....*

Welch, Charles. (1894) *History of the Tower Bridge and of Other Bridges Over the Thames*

Free Books by Charles River Editors

We have brand new titles available for free most days of the week. To see which of our titles are currently free, click on this link.

Discounted Books by Charles River Editors

We have titles at a discount price of just 99 cents everyday. To see which of our titles are currently 99 cents, click on this link.

Made in the USA
Middletown, DE
24 April 2017